The Attributes of

The A

God-

A layman's perspective

(updated 2018 AD)

William Shagbark Hubbell

ISBN 1519585667

ISBN-13: 978-1519585660

Dedication

Now to our God and Father

Be Glory

forever and ever Amen.

(Philippians 4:20 New King James Version Bible)

In essentials, unity;

In non-essentials liberty;

And in all things charity.

(attributed variously to Rupert Medonius,

Count Nicholas Von Zinzedorf of the
Moravian Church and to John Wesley
founder of Methodism.)

Also by William Shagbark Hubbell

- The Shagbark Jokebook Revised

- The Second Shagbark Jokebook

- The Third Shagbark Jokebook

- The fourth Shagbark Jokebook

- QS2200 - a novel

- The Other Hotel - a novel

- On the Grid - a novel

- 7711- a memoir of Beaux Arts 1970

- Sunset Song- Poetry

Contents

Acknowledgements

The quote "In essentials unity…"
Was found on
http://forum.quoteland.com/eve/forums/a/tpc/f/9
/9191541/m/4601000351

Except as noted bible quotations are from <u>The New
Living Bible Translation</u> ©1997 Tyndale House
Publisher
"Power all Power Surely is Thine" from the hymn
"<u>Have Thine Own Way Lord</u>" by Adelaide Pollard
1907
"God Rest ye Merry Gentlemen" was written
by someone lost in history.

Information on Nineveh Region from
http://christianaid.org/News/2014/mir20141204.aspx
and the Global Prayer Digest December 2015 page 64
subscriptions @frontierventures.org

Introduction

Having come into a relationship with God at about age ten I have seen over the last half century how he has worked in my life and the lives of others.

I have never attended any seminary yet I still recognize the major attributes of God and wish to pass on what I think he is like.

Some of this I obtained from Churches I attended along the way and some of it I attended from my own study; but none of it would have been evident to me without the Holy Spirit of God working in and through me; for the things of the Spirit are spiritually discerned.

I do not ask that anyone agree with all I have said here in this work, But I would ask you to prayerfully consider them and show you what are essentials here and what is just Mr. Hubbell's opinion.

Chapter One
Creativity

Christians do not agree about how long it took to make the universe, but one thing we do agree on is that he is the one who did it. He in fact made something out of nothing because in the beginning that was all there was to work with.

After thinking up and putting into effect the laws of physics he used them to order his newly created matter. These molecules eventually became galaxies, stars and planets.

I further think he used natural law to make protozoa, then plant life, fish, amphibians, dinosaurs and a whole other host of living things.

Man however is another story. Man was made miraculously. In mans case he does not say let the Earth, or let the water bring forth man. Instead he says let **us make man**. This level of involvement by the trinity is a level of involvement not seen previously. The statement continues "make man in our image" Our soul and our minds were patterned after him. And once the body was complete God breathed into it the breath of life.

I do not believe that this means that prior to the existence of man God looked outwardly like us. What it does mean is that we have attributes like creativity that once only belonged to God. The cars we drive, the furnaces that heat our homes, the printing press that put out this book are all expressions of our creativity.
Of course there will always be a quantitative difference because we are mortal finite beings and He is an infinite eternal God.

As our astronomers find more creative ways to see farther into the cosmos we are only catching a glimpse into what God did when he created it.

When our microscopes and tools of biology and anatomy figure out the way living cells operate they are seeing the complexity of his creation.

When quantum theorists delve into the sub-atomic particles they are also seeing that creativity is not just about what you see but also about what you don't see.

$$E=mc^2$$

Chapter 2
The All Powerful

How does one describe the power of God? The most powerful thing man has devised is the Hydrogen Bomb unleashing megatons of energy. But such power is commonplace in every star. And God created them in numbers so vast as top boggle the mind. A single comet hitting the earth could do more damage than any hydrogen bomb in our arsenals. Lucifer had control of such power as the "Light Bringer" but even his power was no match for God.

On a more personal note we have terrorist groups trying to make the enemies of their group feel powerless yet an old Christmas Carol says:

"God rest ye merry gentlemen; let nothing you dismay. Remember Christ your savior was born on Christmas Day; To save us all from Satan's power when we had gone astray- O tidings of comfort and Joy." When this was written over five hundred years ago the English language had different meanings for some words. A more modern version would say: God keep you firm, God's mighty child, let nothing you dismay. Remember Christ our savior was born on Christmas day. His birth there promised all of us freedom from our sin. That's a newsflash of comfort and joy, comfort and joy. Yes a newsflash of comfort and joy."

It is like Paul told the Corinthians:

"If God is for us, who can ever be against us? What then shall we say to these things? If God is for us who can be against us? He who did not spare his own son, but delivered him up for us all, how shall He not with him also freely give us all things? Who shall bring a charge against God's elect? It is God who justifies. Who is he who condemns? It is Christ who died, and furthermore I also risen, who is even at the right hand of God, who also makes intercession for us. Who shall separate us from the love of Christ? Shall tribulation, or distress, or persecution, or famine, or nakedness, or peril, or sword? ...in all these things we are more than conquerors through him who loved us. For I am persuaded that neither death nor life, nor angels nor principalities, nor powers, nor nor things present nor things to come, nor height nor depth, nor any other created thing shall be able to separate us from the love of God which is in Christ Jesus our Lord."

(Romans 8:31-39 New King James Version)

Through the ages both men and angels have tried to rival God, but their power is limited while God is a being of infinite power.

The book of Job says:

God stretches the northern sky over empty space and hangs the Earth on nothing...the foundations of the heavens tremble at his rebuke. By his power the sea became calm, by his skill he crushed chaos and made the heavens beautiful.... These are some of the things he does- merely a whisper of his power."   (Job 26:5-14)

An old hymn says "Power all power surely is thine, touch me and heal me Savior divine."

At one point a man was unable to get off his pallet and Jesus told him "your sins are forgiven. " He was showing that his power extended not only over physical problems but included spiritual ones also. The religious leaders missed the point and so he went on to say to the man "stand up, take your mat and go home- you are healed. Then the man jumped up and went home." (Matthew 9:2-8)

When John the Baptist was sitting in jail and began to doubt the power of Jesus - word was sent to him "Go back and tell John what you have seen and heard- the blind see, the lame walk, lepers are cured, the deaf hear, dead are raised to life, and the good news is preached to the poor" (Luke 7:22-24)

This power to do miracles was just a small sample of God's power, but it was a sign to mankind that here was one with the power to overcome sin completely. A power that would be shown in the death and resurrection of Christ. A power that at the end of time will subdue all resistance.

In the last days he shall come as one on a white horse, followed by an extremely large army of believers. It is written:

"From his mouth came a sharp sword and with it he struck down the nations; he ruled them with an iron rod, and he trod the winepress of the wrath of Almighty God." (Rev. 19:11-15)

Although this has yet to come- John saw it as

if it had already become a past event, for God's power is so great it even transcends time.

Chapter 3.
The All Knowing

Near the end of the first chapter of John's gospel there is this story:

Philip went off to look for Nathanael and told him "We have found who Moses and the Prophets wrote about. His name is Jesus, the son of Joseph from Nazareth."

Nathaniel was very skeptical that anyone noteworthy could come out of Nazareth but he came to see for himself.

As he approached Jesus said "here comes an honest man- a true son of Israel!"

"Teacher, how do you know about me?" Nathaniel asked. And Jesus replied:

I could see you under the fig tree before Philip found you."

Nathaniel replied "Teacher, you are the son of God- the king of Israel !"

Jesus asked him do you believe all this just because I said I saw you under a fig tree? You shall see greater things than this."

(John 1:45-50)

There was a political cartoon a while back where someone forgot a password on a computer file, so they called up a Russian hacker. They had been told that the hackers knew everything. In their case it was a bit of an exaggeration.   Government intelligence agencies may go to great lengths to know as much as possible, but even they fall short sometimes. God however is infinite, and his knowledge is complete. It includes what it was like before time itself began, to the definite answer of what the future holds for each of the trillions of events that have yet to occur. His knowledge stretches from how to make a Higgs Boson to how many molecules there are in the universe. God wrote the laws of Physics and scientists today are just getting an overview of what he knew from the beginning. It is my opinion that God knew in advance that man, although created in his image could not survive in a world populated by dinosaurs and thought up a way to get rid of them before man was even created. God also knew from day one that he would need to pay a price to redeem man from sin.

Chapter 4.
The All Seeing

While on vacation once I visited a cavern in Chattanoga , Tennessee. When the guide was satisfied that the last elevator of tourists had made their way into position he turned out all the lights. It was so dark you could not see your own hands.

Companies are always coming up with new forms of yard lights because they believe it will discourage crime. Now while it is true that people will be less likely to spot criminals in dim light, this is not true of God.

An infinite God sees everything and everyone, Whether you are in a lead vault or even thousands of feet underground in a cavern with the lights out. Lead may stop superman from seeing but it does not stop God.

Now some may be saying about now "If God sees all the evil in the world why doesn't he do something about it. To answer that Jesus once gave a parable.

"The kingdom of Heaven is like a field where a farmer had planted good seed. That night as everyone slept an enemy crept in and planted weeds among the wheat. When the crop began to grow and produce grain the weeds also grew. The farmer's servants came and told him: Sir, that field that you planted with good seed is full of weeds.   An enemy has done it! The farmer replied.

Shall we pull out the weeds they asked.

No, he replied, you will hurt the wheat if you do that. Let both grow until the harvest, then I will tell the harvesters to sort out the weeds and burn them and to put the wheat in the barn. (Matthew 13:24-30) The servants in that story did not need to tell the farmer about the weeds, he had already seen them and had decided to wait before dealing with them. Likewise God sees all the evil in the world today. Just because he is letting it happen does not mean they will get away with it. When the final judgment comes then he will make it right.

God has seen the death of every martyr. And he will see every deed done by Antichrist during the coming tribulation, but because he is a just God he always wants witnesses before passing judgment. Man can only see what happens if he was present at the event or sees a video of it played out later. God does not have this limitation. He is an infinite God and can watch everywhere at the same time. And that applies to good deeds too. Matthew wrote in his gospel : "Your father who sees in secret will reward you openly.

What God sees from his point of view isn't always what you might expect as shown when Samuel was sent to anoint one of Jesse's sons to replace Saul as King of Israel.

God told the prophet "go fill your horn with olive oil and go to Bethlehem. Find a man there named Jesse, for I have selected one of his sons to be my new king.." Samuel thought maybe is is the firstborn son. Samuel was wrong.

"Samuel took one look at Eliab and thought surely this must be the Lord's anointed one. But God told him don't judge by appearance or height- I have rejected him…People judge by appearances but the Lord looks at man's thoughts and intentions. (I Samuel 16)

Later when David sinned and tried to cover it up God saw what he had done and sent a prophet to confront him. David, like some of the wicked kings later, could have had the man thrown in prison but instead he repented and told the prophet "I have sinned against the Lord. (II Samuel 12:13)

David knew that it was useless to try to hide

sin from the God who sees all things.

Chapter 5
Our Compassionate God

The book of Jonah is primarily known for a man who was swallowed by a big fish. Now while it is a miracle living three days in the belly of a fish what the book is really about is how quick God turns from wrath to mercy.

Jonah would never have been in that predicament if he had obeyed God in the first place. Yet, as soon as he repented God showed compassion and had the fish spit him out. The real message however was not just showing compassion on one man but to a whole city. Jonah knew what a violent people the city of Nineveh was and he was going to enjoy watching them get destroyed ; but instead look what happened

The King of Nineveh dressed in sackcloth and sat in a heap of ashes. The king sent out this decree: No one may eat or drink. Everyone is required to wear sackcloth and pray earnestly to God. He also said everyone must turn from their evil ways and stop all violence.

This was the last thing Jonah wanted to see happen, but it was exactly what God wanted and as soon as God saw their repentant hearts he cancelled the destruction.

The book ends with the words " Nineveh has

more than 120,000 people living in spiritual
darkness, not to mention all the animals there.
Shouldn't I feel sorry for so great a city?"

Christ himself referred to the prophet Jonah
and the repentance of Nineveh. When he said
"for as Jonah was three days and three nights
in the belly of the great fish, so I , the son of
man will be three days and nights in the heart
of the Earth." (Matthew 12:40)

And such was the compassion of Christ that
after the physical, emotional , and spiritual
agony of atoning for mankind's sin rather than
resting for three days in heaven he instead
went to the heart of the Earth to assist those
who had died anticipating his birth.

Within our generation, the province of
Nineveh was again under the control of
violent jihadists. But according to the Global
Prayer digest and other sources, atrocities by

ISIS softened the hearts of Muslims to Christianity, and evangelistic techniques and technologies proved effective. The real reason, however, according to missionaries, that there was a spike in conversions is that Muslims are finding for themselves that God is real.

In the war torn regions of the middle east displaced people are learning from native aid workers and other sources about the love of Christ and tent churches are sprouting like mushrooms.

Yes, there is evil. Yes sometimes justice is delayed but this does not mean God lacks compassion. His compassion may not always be evident but nevertheless it is there.

6 THE GLORIOUS ONE

The Milky Way on a full dark night is glorious. Sunrise on Tierra Del Fuego when the weather is right is glorious.

Autumns splendor in Tahquamenon Park is glorious. All of these show the physical glory of God. I've been there. On a beach with no security lights watching as the center of our galaxy rose above the Gulf of Mexico. On a ship docked on the Beagle Channel with the pale rays of morning getting more glorious by the second. On a country road canopied with trees at the height of their color. I was there and I can tell you it was glorious.

But I can tell you there is another kind of glory. A Spiritual glory. As the Apostle Paul put it:

"For God knew his people in advance and he chose them to be like his son… and having chosen them He called them to come to him. And he gave them right standing with himself and promised them his glory."

(Romans 8:29-30)

This is a spiritual glory promised to the redeemed of all ages. And the more Christians are added to that number, the greater the weight of glory.

In this life we faintly reflect that glory; but in the life to come we will see its full brilliance.

At the end of time Christ shall return to Jerusalem. He will be seated on a white horse followed by a great army and the sight of them will be so glorious that the rocks themselves will sing forth his praise and make a way into the city.

And yet there is a more glorious event. In Rev. it states " And I saw a new heaven and a new Earth…

Then he who sat on the throne said: Behold I make all things new. And he said to me (*not me personally but rather the author of Rev.*)

Write , for these words are faithful and true. And he said It is done. I am the Alpha and the Omega, the beginning and the end. I will give of the fountain of waters of life freely to him who thirsts

This was the holy Jerusalem descending out of heaven from God , having the glory of

God... The city had no need of sun or moon to shine in it for the glory of God illuminated it. ...and the nations who are saved shall walk in its light, and the kings of the Earth will bring their glory and honor into it.   (Rev. 21)

The all knowing, all powerful, all seeing creator of the universe shall do this. He will do it as a function of his compassion toward us and it will be glorious. I hope you have right standing with him. I hope I will see you there.

Jesus said:

"I assure you that those who listen to my message and believe in God the one who sent me shall have eternal life.

...the time is coming, in fact is here now, when the dead shall hear my voice- the voice of the Son of God- and those who listen will live." (Matthew 5: 24-25)

Are you listening to him? Have you received the salvation he is offering now. Nobody in these dangerous times is promised tomorrow.

Accept his plan of Salvation now. And may God richly bless you as you share in his divine attributes.

The ABC's of Salvation

A. Admit God exists

In order to develop any kind of relationship with God one must first admit that God exists and that he has standards for behavior, that are based on his revealed will and not on human culture.

Once you do that you will see that people miss the mark of reaching his standards. This we call sin.

B. Believe his plan

The good news is that the all knowing God knew in advance that people would miss the mark and so he made a way.

As it is written in the gospel of John

"For God so loved the world that he gave his only begotten son that everyone that believes in him will not perish but have Eternal life." (John 3:16)

As Paul told the Romans:

" We are made right when we trust Jesus Christ to take away our sins, and we can be saved that way, no matter who we are or what we have done ...we are made right with God

when we believe that Christ shed his blood,
sacrificing his life for us. (Romans 3:22,25)

The All powerful God showed he was in this
plan by raising Christ from the dead. And
you can get in on this offer. As he said in the
first chapter of Johns Gospel :
But to all who believed in him and accepted
him he gave the right to become children of
God! They are reborn!" (John 1: 12-13)

C. Confess Jesus is Lord

To get in on this put your faith in him and
ask him to come into your life.
As it says later in Romans: "For if you confess
with your mouth and believe in your heart
that Jesus is Lord… that God raised him
from the dead then you **will** be saved.
It is by believing in your heart that you are
made right with God and it is by confessing
with your mouth that you are saved."
(Romans 10:9)
Since God is always present he will hear your
prayer. Tell him you are ready to do things
his way. That you turn from your sin and
with his help you receive him as Savior and
Lord.
Faster than a hyperlink he will come into

your life and save you.
I hope you have done this. It is a perilous
time we are living in. But heaven awaits us
when this life is finished, if you are his.

BIBLE READING PLAN

As I said in the previous chapter we are
living in perilous times. But we are not alone.
We have Christ and we have other Christians.
Find a Bible believing Church and become
part of its body. Learn to be a disciple of
Christ and walk daily with him. Every
Christian should make Prayer and Bible
reading part of every day.

Prayer is when you talk to your heavenly
father. Bible Reading and study is when you
learn what God wants our lives to be like.
You may get impulses to action but not every
impulse is from God. So you must test it
against scripture. I Timothy says:

2 TIM 3:16–17
**ALL SCRIPTURE IS GIVEN BY INSPIRATION OF GOD,
AND IS PROFITABLE FOR DOCTRINE, FOR REPROOF, FOR
CORRECTION, FOR INSTRUCTION IN RIGHTEOUSNESS,
THAT THE MAN OF GOD MAY BE COMPLETE,
THOROUGHLY EQUIPPED FOR EVERY GOOD WORK.**
NKJV

But the Bible is a big volume and takes a
Person awhile to even read "All Scripture"
much less study it. So plans have been
concocted to subdivide it into daily readings
so after 365 days you have read the whole
thing. What follows is one of those plans
which I put together for my own daily study.
I hope you find it as helpful as I do.

Here are a couple abbreviations I use
O.T. =Old Testament
EOC= end of chapter

January				
	O.T. history & prophecy	O.T. poetry and wisdom		New Testament
Jan 01	Genesis 1-3	Proverbs 1:1-9		Matthew 1
02	Genesis 4-6	Prov. 1: 10-19		Matthew 2
03	Gen. 7-9	Prov. 1:20-eoc		Matthew 3
04	Gen. 10-12	Psalm 1		Matthew 4
05	Gen. 13-15	Prov. 2:1-7		Matt 5:1-26
06	Gen. 16-17	Prov. 2:8-15		Matt 5:27-eoc
07	Gen. 18-19	Prov. 2:16- eo		Matt. 6:1-18
08	Gen. 20-22	Psalm 2		Matt 6:19-eoc
09	Gen. 23-24	Prov. 3: 1-12		Matt.7
10	Gen. 25-26	Prov. 3:13-26		Matt.8:1-17
11	Gen. 27-28	Prov. 3:27-eoc		Matt 8:18-eoc

12	Gen. 29-30	Prov. 4:1-10	Matt.9:1-23
13	Gen.31-32	Proverbs 4: 11-19	Matt.9:24-eoc
14	Gen. 33-35	Proverbs: 4:20-eoc	Matt.10:1-20
15	Gen. 36-38	Prov. 5: 1-13	Matt.10:21-eoc
16	Gen. 39-40	Prov. 5: 14-19	Matt.11:1-eoc
17	Gen.36-38	Prov. 5: 20-eoc	Matt.12:1-21
18	Gen.	Prov. 6:1-6	Matt.12:22-eoc
19	Gen.	Prov. 6:7-12	Matt.13:1-30
20	Gen. 36-38	Proverbs 7	Matt.13:31-eoc
21	Exodus 1-3	Proverbs 8	Matt. 14:1-21
22	Exodus 4-6	Psalm 3.4	Matt.14:21-eoc
23	Exodus 7-9	Psalm 5.6	Matt.15:1-20
24	Exodus 10-11	Prov. 9	Matt.15:21-eoc
25	Exodus 12-13	Psalm 7,	Matthew 16
26	Exodus 14-15	Psalm 8	Matthew 17

27	Exodus 16-18		Psalm 9-10		Matt. 18:1-30
28	Exodus 19-20		Proverbs 10		Matthew 18:21-eoc
29	Ex. 21-22		Psalm 11-12		Matthew 19
30	Ex. 23-24		Psalm 13, 14		Matt. 20:1-19
31	Exodus 25,26		Proverbs 11		Matthew: 20:20-eoc

February					
	O.T. history & prophecy		O.T. poetry and wisdom		New Testament
Feb 01	Exodus 27-28		Prov. 12: 1-12		Matthew 21:1-21
02	Exo. 29-31		Psalm 15-16		Matt. 21:22-eoc
03	Exo. 32-33		Psalm 17		Matt. 22:1-20
04	Exo. 34-35		Prov.12:13-eoc		Matt. 22:21-eoc
05	Exo. 36-38		Psalm 18		Matt. 23: 1-22
06	Exo. 39-40		Psalm 19-20		Matt. 23:23-eoc
07	Leviticus 1-3		Proverbs 13		Matthew 24:1-28
08	Lev. 4-5		Psalm 21		Matt. 24:29-eoc
09	Lev. 6-7		Psalm 22		Matt. 25: 1-30
10	Lev. 8-10		Prov. 14		Matt. 25: 31-eoc
11	Lev. 11-12		Psalm 23		Matt: 26:

12	Lev. 13-14	Psalm 24	Matt. 26
13	Lev. 15-16	Prov. 15	Matt.
14	Lev. 15,16	Psalm 25	Matt. 27:1-26
15	Lev. 17	Psalm 26	Matt. 27:27-49
16	Lev. 18-19	Prov. 16	Matt. 27:50-eoc
17	Lev. 20-21	Psalm 27	Matt. 28:1-15
18	Lev. 22-23	Psalm 28	Matt. 28:16-end
19	Lev. 24-25	Prov. 17	Mark 1
20	Lev. 26-27	Psalm 29	Mark 2
21	Num. 1-3	Psalm 30	Mark 3
22	Num.4-6	Prov. 18	Mark 4:1-20
23	Num. 7-8	Psalm 31	Mark 4:21-eoc
24	Num. 9-11	Psalm 32	Mark 5:1-20
25	Num. 12-14	Prov. 19	Mark 5:21-eoc
26	Num. 15-16	Psalm 33	Mark:6:1-29
27	Num.17-20	Psalm 34	Mark 6:30-eoc
28	Num.20-22	Prov. 20	Mark 7:1-13

March				
	O.T. history & prophecy		O.T. poetry and wisdom	New Testament
Mar 1	Num. 23-25		Psalm 35	Mark 7:14-eoc
02	Num. 26-27		Prov. 36	Mar 8:1-21
03	Num. 28-30		Prov. 21	Mark 8:22-eoc
04	Num. 31-33		Psalm 37:1-20	Mark 9:1--29
05	Num. 34-36		Psalm 37:21-eoc	Mark 9: 30-eoc
06	Deut. 1-2		Prov. 22	Mark 10: 1-20
07	Deut. 3-4		Psalm 38	Mark 10:21-eoc
08	Deut. 5-7		Psalm 39	Mark 11:1-18
09	Deut. 8-10		Proverbs. 23:1-18	Mark 11:19-eoc
10	Deut. 11-13		Psalm 40	Mark 12:1-27
11	Deut. 14-16		Psalm 41	Mark 12:28-eoc
12	Deut. 17-19		Proverbs. 23:19-eoc	Mark 13: 1-20
13	Deut. 20-22		Psalm 42	Mark 13:21-eoc

The Attributes of God   William Shagbark Hubbell

14	Deut 23-25		Psalm 43		Mark 14:1-26
15	Deut. 26-27		Proverbs. 24:1-12		Mark:14: 27-53
16	Deut. 28-29		Psalm 44		Mark 14 54-eoc
17	Deut. 30-31		Psalm 45		Mark 15:1-25
18	Deut. 32- 34		Proverbs. 24:13-eoc		Mark 15:26- eoc
19	Joshua 1-3		Psalm 46		Mark 16
20	Joshua 4-6		Psalm 47		Luke 1: 1-38
21	Joshua 7-9		Proverbs. 25:1-15		Luke 1: 39-58
22	Josh. 10-12		Psalm 48		Luke:59-eoc
23	Josh. 13-15		Psalm 49		Luke 2: 1-20
24	Josh. 16-18		Proverbs. 25:16-eoc		Luke 2: 21-40
25	Josh. 19-21		Psalm 50		Luke 2:41- eoc
26	Josh. 22-24		Psalm 51		Luke 3
27	Judges 1-3		Proverbs. 26:1-15		Luke 4:1-30
28	Judges 4-6		Psalm 52		Luke 4:31-eoc

29	Judges 7-8		Psalm 53		Luke 5:1-16
30	Judges 9-10		Proverbs. 26:16-eoc		Luke 5: 17-eoc
31	Jud. 11-12		Psalm 54		Luke 6:1-26

April				
	O.T. history & prophecy	O.T. poetry and wisdom		New Testament
Apr 01	Judges 13-15	Psalm 55		Luke 6:27-eoc
02	Judges 16-18	Prov. 27:1-16		Luke 7:1-25
03	Judges 19-21	Psalm 56		Luke 7:26-eoc
04	Ruth 1-2	Psalm 57		Luke 8:1-25
05	Ruth 3-4	Prov. 27:17-eoc		Luke8:26-eoc
06	I Sam. 1-4	Psalm 58		Luke 9:1-17
07	I Sam. 5-7	Psalm 59		Luke 9:18-36
08	I Sam. 8-11	Prov. 28: 1-15		Luke 9:37-eoc
09	I Sam. 12-14	Psalm 60		Luke 10:1-24
10	I Sam. 15-16	Psalm 61		Luke 10:25-eoc
11	I Sam. 17-187	Prov. 28: 16-eoc		Luke 11:1-28
12	I Sam. 19-21	Psalm 62		Luke 11:29-eoc
13	I Sam. 22-24	Psalm 63		Luke 12:1-31

14	I Sam. 25-26	Prov. 29:1-13		Luke 12:32-eoc:
15	I Sam.27-29	Psalm 64		Luke 13:1-17
16	I Sam. 30-31	Psalm 65		Luke13:18-eoc
17	II Sam. 1-2	Prov. 29:14-eoc		Luke14:1-14
18	II Sam. 3-5	Psalm 66		Luke 14:15-eoc
19	II Sam. 6-8	Proverbs 30: 1-5		Luke 15:1-10
20	II Sam. 9-11	Psalm 67		Luke 15:11-eoc
21	II Sam. 12-13	Prov. 30: 6-10		Luke 16
22	II Sam. 14-15	Psalm 68		Luke 17:1-19
23	II Sam. 16-18	Psalm 69		Luke 17:20-eoc
24	II Sam. 19-20	Prov. 30: 11-eoc		Luke 1 8:1-23
25	II Sam. 21-22	Psalm 70		Luke 18:24-eoc
26	II Sam. 23-24	Psalm 71		Luke 19: 1-27
27	I Kings:1-2	Prov. 31:1-9		Luke 19:28-eoc
28	I Kings 3-5	Psalm 72		Luke 20:1-26
29	I Kings 6-7	Psalm 73		Luke 20-:27-eoc
30	I Kings 8-9	Prov. 31:10-eoc		Luke 21:1-19

May			
	O.T. history & prophecy	Poetry & Wisdom	New Testament
May 01	I Kings 10-11	Eccles. 1	Luke 21:20-eoc
02	I Kings 12-13	Psalm 74	Luke 22:1-20
03	I Kings 14-15	Psalm 75	Luke 22:21-45
04	I Kings 16-18	Eccles. 2	Luke 22:46-eoc
05	I Kings 19-20	Psalm 76	Luke 23:1-25
06	I Kings 21-22	Psalm 77	Luke 23:26-eoc
07	II Kings 1-3	Eccles. 3	Luke 24:1-35
08	II Kings 4-6	Psalm 78	Luke 24:36-eoc
09	II Kings 7-9	Psalm 79	John 1:1-28
10	II Kings 10-12	Eccles. 4	John 1:29-eoc
11	II Kings 13-14	Psalm 80	John 2
12	II Kings 15-16	Psalm 81	John 3: 1-18
13	II Kings 17-18	Eccles. 5	John 3:19- eoc
14	II Kings 19-21	Psalm 82	John 4: 1-30
15	II Kings 22-23	Psalm 83	John 4:31-eoc

16	II Kings 24-25		Eccles. 6		John 5: 1-24
17	I Chron. 1-3		Psalm 84		John 5: 25-eoc
18	I Chron. 4-6		Psalm 85		John 6:1-21
19	I Chron. 7-9		Eccles. 7		John 6:22-44
20	I Chron. 10-12		Psalm 86		John 6: 45-eoc
21	I Chron. 13-15		Psalm 87		John 7: 1-27
22	I Chron. 16-18		Eccles. 8		John 7:28-eoc
23	I Chron. 19-21		Psalm 88		John 8:1-27
24	I Chron. 22-24		Psalm 89		John8:28-eoc
25	I Chron. 25-27		Psalm 90		John 9:1-23
26	I Chron. 28-29		Eccles. 9		John 9:24-eoc
27	II Chron. 1-3		Psalm 91		John 10:1-23
28	II Chron. 4-6		Psalm 92		John 10: 24-eoc
29	II Chron. 7-9		Eccles. 10		John 11: 1-29
30	II Chron. 10-12		Psalm 93		John 11:30-eoc
31	II Chron. 13-14		Psalm 94		John 12:1-11

June			
	O.T. history & prophecy	O.T. poetry and wisdom	New Testament
June 1	II Chron. 15-16	Eccles. 11	John 12:12-eoc
02	II Chron. 17- 18	Psalm 95	John13: 1-20
03	II Chron. 19-20	Psalm 96	John 13: 21-eoc
04	II Chron 21-22	Eccles. 12	John 14
05	II Chron. 23	Psalm 97	John 15
06	II chron. 24	Psalm 98	John 16
07	II Chron. 25	Prov. 1:1-10	John 17
08	II Chron. 26	Psalm 99	John 18:1-18
09	II Chron. 27	Psalm100, Psalm 101	John 18:19-eoc
10	II Chron. 28	Prov. 1:11-21	John 19: 1-30
11	II Chron. 29	Psalm 102	John 19:31-eoc
12	II Chron 30	Psalm 103	John 20
13	II Chron. 31	Prov. 1:22-eoc	John 21
14	II Chron. 32	Psalm 104	Acts 1

15	II Chron. 33		Psalm 105		Acts 2:1-14
16	II Chron 34		Prov. 2: 1-11		Acts 2:15-eoc
17	II Chron 35		Psalm 106		Acts 3
18	II Chron. 36		Psalm 107		Acts 4: 1-32
19	Ezra 1		Prov. 2:12-eoc		Acts 4: 33-eoc
20	Ezra 2		Psalm 108		Acts 5:1-32
21	Ezra 3		Psalm 109		Acts 5:33-eoc
22	Ezra 4		Prov. 3:1-10		Acts 6
23	Ezra 5		Psalm 110		Acts 7:1-18
24	Ezra 6		Psalm 111		Acts 7:19-53
25	Ezra 7		Prov.3:11-20		Acts 7:54-eoc
26	Ezra 8		Psalm 112		Acts 8:1-25
27	Ezra 9		Psalm 113		Acts 8:26-eoc
28	Ezra 10		Prov. 3:21-eoc		Acts 9:1-22
29	Nehemiah 1		Psalm 114		Acts 9:23-eoc
30	Nehemiah 2		Psalm 115		Acts 10: 1-23

July			
	O.T. history & prophecy	O.T. poetry and wisdom	New Testament
July 01	Nehemiah 3	Prov 4:1-10	Acts 10:24-eoc
02	Nehemiah 4	Psalm 116	Acts 11
03	Nehemiah 5	Psalm 117	Acts 12:1-13:3
04	Nehemiah 6	Prov 4:11-19	Acts 13:4-30
05	Nehemiah 7	Psalm 118	Acts 13:31-eoc
06	Nehemiah 8	Psalm 119:1-8	Acts 14
07	Nehemiah 9	Prov. 4:20-eoc	Acts 15:1-21
08	Nehemiah 10	Ps 119:9-16	Acts 15: 22-eoc
09	Nehemiah 11	Ps 119:17-24	Acts 16:1-23
10	Nehemiah 12	Prov. 5: 1-13	Acts 16:24-eoc
11	Nehemiah 13	Ps 119 :25-32	Acts 17:1-15
12	Esther	Ps 119:33-40	Acts 17:16-eoc
13	Esther	Prov. 5: 14-19	Acts 18
14	Esther	Ps 119:41-48	Acts 19:1-20
15	Esther	Ps 119 : 49-56	Acts 19:21-eoc

16	Esther 7-9		Ps 119: 49-56		Acts 20:1-16
17	Job 1-2		Prov. 5: 20-eoc		Acts 20:17-eoc
18	Job 3-4		Ps 119:57-64		Acts 21:1-17
19	Job 5-6		Ps 119:65-72		Acts 21:18-eoc
20	Job 7-8		Ps 119:73-80		Acts 22:1-15
21	Job 9		Ps 119:81-88		Acts 22:16-eoc
22	Job 10		Prov. 6:22-eoc		Acts23
23	Job 11		Ps 119:89-96		Acts 24
24	Job 12		Ps 119:97-104		Acts 25
25	Job 13		Prov. 7		Acts 26
26	Job 14		Ps 119:105-112		Acts 27
27	Job 15		Ps 119:113-120		Acts 28
28	Job 16		Proverbs 8		Romans 1: 1-15
29	Job 17		Ps 119:121-128		Romans 1:16-eoc
30	Job 18		Ps 119:129-136		Romans 2
31	Job 19-20		Prov. 9:1-9		Romans 3

August		
O.T. history & prophecy	O.T. poetry and wisdom	New Testament
Aug 01	Job 21	Ps 119:137-144	Romans 4
02	Job 22	Ps119:145-152	Romans 5
03	Job 23	Prov. 9:10-eo	Romans 6
04	Job 24	Ps119:153-160	Romans 7
05	Job 25	Ps119:161-168	Romans 8:1-21
06	Job 26	Prov. 10	Romans 8:22-eoc
07	Job 27	Ps 119:169-17	Romans 9:1-15
08	Job 28	Psalm 120	Romans 9:16-eoc
09	Job 29	Prov. 11	Romans 10
10	Job 30-31	Psalm 121	Romans 11:1-18
11	Job 32-33	Psalm 122	Romans 11:19-eoc

12	Job 34		Prov:12: 1-13	Romans 12
13	Job 35-36		Psalm 123	Romans 13
14	Job 37-39		Psalm 124	Romans 14
15	Job 40-42		Prov 12:14-eoc	Rom 15:1-13
16	Song-of-Songs 1-2		Psalm 125	Rom 15:14-eoc
17	Song-of-Songs 3-4		Psalm 126	Romans 16
18	Song-of-Songs 5-6		Prov. 13	I Corinth. 1
19	Song-of-Songs 7-8		Psalm 127	I Corinth. 2
20	Isa 1-2		Psalm 128	I Corinth. 3
21	Isa 3-4		Prov.14	I Corinth. 4
22	Isa 5-6		Psalm 129	I Corinth. 5
23	Isa 7-8		Psalm 130	I Corinth. 6
24	Isa 9-10		Prov. 15	I Corinth 7:1-19

.... continued next page..........................

25	Isa 11-12		Psalm 131		I Cor. 7:20-eoc
26	Isa 13-14		Psalm 132		I Corinth 8
27	Isa 15-16		Prov. 16		I Corinth 9
28	Isa 17-18		Psalm 133		I Corinth 10:1-18
29	Isa 19-20		Psalm 134		I Corinthians 10:19-eoc
30	Isa 21-22		Proverb 17		I Corinthians 11:1-16
31	Isa 23-24		Psalm 135		I Corinthians 11:17-eoc

September				
	O.T. history & prophecy		O.T. poetry and wisdom	New Testament
Sep 01	Isa. 25-26		Psalm 136	I Cor. 12
02	Isa. 27-28		Proverb 18	I Cor. 13
03	Isa. 29-30		Psalm 137	I Cor. 14
04	Isa. 31-32		Psalm 138	I Cor. 15
05	Isa. 33-34		Proverb 19	I Cor. 16
06	Isa. 35-36		Psalm 139	II Cor.1
07	Isa. 37-38		Psalm 140	II Cor. 2
08	Isa. 39-40		Proverb 20	II Cor. 3
09	Isa. 41-42		Psalm 141	II Cor. 4
10	Isa. 43-44		Psalm 142	II Cor. 5
11	Isa. 45-46		Proverb 21	II Cor. 6
12	Isa. 47-48		Psalm 143	II Cor. 7
13	Isa. 49-50		Psalm 144	II Cor. 8

14	Isa. 51-52	Prov. 22		II Cor. 9
15	Isa. 53-54	Psalm 145		II Cor. 10
16	Isa. 55-56	Psalm 146		II Cor. 11
17	Isa. 57-58	Prov. 23:1-18		II Cor. 12
18	Isa. 59-60	Psalm 147		II Cor. 13
19	Isa. 61-62	Psalm 149		Galatians 1
20	Isa. 63-64	Prov. 23:19-eoc		Galatians 2
21	Isa. 65-66	Psalm 150		Galatians 3
22	Jer. 1-2	Psalm 1		Galatians 4
23	Jer. 3-4	Prov. 24:1-12		Galatians 5
24	Jer. 5-6	Psalm 2		Galatians 6
25	Jer. 7.8	Psalm 3-4		Ephesians 1
26	Jer. 9-10	Prov. 24:13-eoc		Ephes. 2
27	Jer. 11-12	Psalm 5-6		Ephes. 3
28	Jer. 13-14	Psalm 7		Ephes. 4
29	Jer. 15-16	Prov. 25:1-19		Ephes. 5
30	Jer. 17-18	Psalm 8		Ephes. 6

October			
	O.T. History &	O.T. Poetry & Wisdom	New Testament
Oct.1	Jer. 19-20	Psalm 9	Philippi. 1
02	Jer. 21-22	Prov. 25:16-eoc	Philippi. 2
03	Jer. 23-24	Psalm 10	Philippi. 3
04	Jer. 25-26	Psalm 11	Philippi. 4
05	Jer. 27-28	Prov. 26:1-10	Colossi. 1
06	Jer. 29-30	Psalm 12	Colossi. 2
07	Jer. 31-32	Psalm 13	Colossi. 3
08	Jer. 33-34	Prov. 26:11- eoc	Colossi. 4
09	Jer. 35-36	Psalm 14	I Thess. 1
10	Jer. 37-38	Psalm 15	I Thess. 2
11	Jer. 39	Prov. 27:1-11	I Thess. 3
12	Jer. 40-41	Psalm 16	I Thess. 4
13	Jer. 42-43	Psalm 17	I Thess. 5
14	Jer. 44-45	Prov. 27:1-11	II Thess. 1
15	Jer. 46-47	Psalm 18	II Thess. 2

16	Jer. 48-49		Psalm 19		II Thess. 3
17	Jer. 50-51		Prov. 28:1-13		I Timothy 1
18	Jer. 52		Psalm 20		I Timothy 2
19	Ezek. 1-2		Psalm 21		I Timothy 3
20	Ezek. 3-4		Prov. 28: 14-eoc		I Timothy 4
21	Ezek. 5-6		Psalm 22		I Timothy 5
22	Ezek. 7-8		Psalm 23		I Timothy 6
23	Ezek. 9-10		Prov. 29:1-16		II Tim. 1
24	Ezek.11-12		Psalm 24		II Tim. 2
25	Ezek.13-14		Psalm 25		II Tim. 3
26	Ezek.15-16		Prov. 29:17- eoc		I Tim. 4
27	Ezek.17-18		Psalm 26		Titus 1
28	Ezek.19-20		Psalm 27		Titus 2
29	Ezek.21-22		Proverbs 30		Titus 3
30	Ezek.23-24		Psalm 50		Philemon
31	Ezek.25-26		Psalm 51		Hebrews

November					
	O.T History & Prophecy		O.T. Poetry & Wisdom		New Testament
Nov 01	Ezek. 27-28		Lament 1		Hebrews 1
02	Ezek. 29-30		Lament 2		Hebrews 2
03	Ezek. 31-32		Lament 3		Hebrews 3
04	Ezek. 33-34		Lament 4		Hebrews 2
05	Ezek. 35-36		Lament 5		Hebrews 6
06	Ezek. 37-38		Psalm 68		Hebrews 7
07	Ezek. 39-40		Psalm 69		Hebrews 8
08	Ezek. 41-42		Prov. 31:1-16		Hebrews 9
09	Ezek. 43-44		Psalm 70		Hebrews 10
10	Ezek. 45-46		Psalm 71		Hebrews 11
11	Ezek. 47-48		Proverbs 31:17- end		Hebrews 12
12	Daniel 1-2		Psalm 72		Hebrews 13
13	Daniel 3-4		Psalm 73		James 1

14	Daniel 5-6	Ecclesi one	James 2
15	Daniel 7-8	Psalm 74	James 3
16	Daniel 9-10	Psalm 75	James 4
17	Daniel 11-12	Ecclesi 2	James 5
18	Hosea 1	Psalm 76	I Peter 1
19	Hosea 2-3	Psalm 77	I Peter 2
20	Hosea 4-5	Ecclesi 3	I Peter 3
21	Hosea 6-7	Psalm 78	I Peter 4
22	Hosea 8-9	Psalm 79	I Peter 5
23	Hosea 10-11	Ecclesi 4	II Peter 1
24	Hosea 12-13	Psalm 80	II Peter 2
25	Hosea 14	Psalm 81	II Peter 3
26	Joel 1	Ecclesi 5	I John 1
27	Joel 2-3	Psalm 82	I John 2
28	Amos 1	Psalm 83	I John 3
29	Amos 2-3	Ecclesi 6	I John 4
30	Amos 4-5	Psalm 84	I John 5

December						
	O.T. history & prophecy		O.T. poetry and wisdom		New Testament	
Dec 01	Amos 6-7		Psalm 85		II John	
02	Amos 8-9		Ecclesi 7		III John	
03	Obadiah		Psalm 86		JUDE	
04	Jonah 1-2		Psalm 88		Rev. 1	
05	Jonah 3-4		Ecclesi 8		Rev. 2	
06	Micah 1		Psalm 90		Rev. 3	
07	Micah 2-3		Psalm 92		Rev. 4	
08	Micah 4-5		Ecclesi. 9		Rev. 5	
09	Micah 6-7		Psalm 94		Rev. 6:1-8	
10	Nahum 1		Psalm 95		Rev. 6:9-eoc	
11	Nahum 2-3		Ecclesi. 10		Rev.7	
12	Habak 1		Psalm 96		Rev. 8	
13	Habak 2-3		Psalm 98		Rev. 9	
14	Zeph. 1-2		Ecclesi. 11		Rev. 10	

15	Zeph. 3		Psalm 100		Rev. 11
16	Haggai 1-2		Psalm 101		Rev. 12
17	Zechariah 1		Psalm 102		Rev. 13
18	Zech. 2-3		Ecclesi. 12		Rev. 14
19	Zech. 4-5		Psalm 141		Rev. 15
20	Zech. 6-7		Psalm 142		Rev. 16
21	Zech. 8-9		Prov. 21		Rev. 17:1-8
22	Zech. 10-11		Psalm 143		Rev. 17:9-eoc
23	Zech. 12		Psalm 144		Rev. 18
24	Micah 5:2		Prov. 22		Rev. 19:1-10
25	Isa. 9:6		Psalm 145		Rev. 19:11-
26	Zech 13		Psalm 146		Rev. 20:1-10
27	Zech 14		Proverb 23		Rev. 20:11-eoc
28	Mal. 1		Psalm 147		Rev 21:1-13
29	Mal.2		Psalm 148		Rev. 21:14-eoc
30	Mal. 3		Psalm 149		Rev. 22:1-9
31	Mal. 4		Psalm 150		Rev. 22:10 to end

The Photographs

The Cover

Photograph of a painting done by the author in the previous century.

Chapter One:

Autos parked west of Grand River plant of General Motors; located next to Interstate 496 in downtown Lansing, Michigan. Photo taken December 2015 by the author

Chapter Two:

The Michigan State Library and Museum

Photo taken September 2015 by the author

Chapter Three:

Albert Einstein was the first to figure out how much

power would be gained by converting matter into energy. He expressed it in this well known equation

Energy equals mass times the speed of light squared.

Chapter Four

This is the Author's version of the All Seeing Eye.

The Latin would roughly translate: God sees all things

Chapter Five

A plaque on the balcony of South Church of Lansing

Photo taken December 2015 by the author.

Chapter Six

Autumn leaves by the Grand River in Lansing Michigan

Photo taken October 2011 by the author.

About the Author

The Photo above was taken at South Church of Lansing where the author is a member

William Hubbell was born in Lansing Michigan in 1947. In 1970, he lived among the hippies at Beaux Arts in Pinellas Park Florida Where he lived among the hippies and showed them God's love. Those days are related in the book _7711_. He has since worked in the states of Michigan, Florida, and Texas.

He has used the pen name shagbark since 2001 when he began writing articles for h2g2.com

William lives with his wife and two cats in Lansing Michigan.

CPSIA information can be obtained
at www.ICGtesting.com
Printed in the USA
BVHW041915080422
633814BV00019B/203

9 781519 585660